I0087978

A Handbook for

RESCUE SQUADS

Prepared by Training Section

U. S. OFFICE OF CIVILIAN DEFENSE

U. S. Government Printing Office, December 1941, Washington, D. C.

PREFACE

This is one of a series of civilian defense handbooks prepared by the United States Office of Civilian Defense. The purpose of each handbook is to instruct the individual enrolled civilian defense worker in his duties and to serve as a manual for reference.

The measures for safeguarding civilians against the effects of air attack, which are described in the following pages, have become a necessary part of the defensive organization of any country open to air attack.

Every State and municipality should take such legal or administrative action as may be necessary to provide for the organization, direction, and training of its Rescue Service.

F. H. LaGuardia,
U. S. Director Civilian Defense.

Washington, D. C.
December 1941.

CONTENTS

CONTENTS—*Cont.*

In Regard to the

RESCUE SERVICE

War from the air and widespread bombing of civilian populations brings with it the problem of extricating persons trapped under debris. Such people, though trapped, may be unharmed except for nervous shock; they may be casualties; or they may be dead. It is the primary duty of the Rescue Squad to save them—the dead as well as the living when it can be done without further risk to life.

In performing this work the Rescue Party may be concerned with:

First Aid.
Incendiary-Bomb Control.
Decontamination.
Urgent Shoring and Demolition.
Utilities—Gas and Water Mains.

In London, where the effect of raiding has tested the rescue squads more severely than any other service, with the possible exception of the fire departments, it has been found that rescue work, in addition to being long, dangerous, and hard, must be performed with *speed* and *care*.

Speed.—Because so long as there is the slightest possibility that a trapped victim is alive, no effort must be spared to accelerate his rescue.

Care.—Because lack of proper precautions may cause landslides, falling debris, or shift of debris in such manner as to kill those trapped.

Steady and continued work also is necessary. It may frequently be from 4 days to a week or even more before all the bodies have been found after an extensive raid. It is not unusual that tunneling and burrowing proceed for 24 hours before the trapped victim is reached.

Such work requires persistence, but every member of a Rescue Squad knows that—

THERE IS TRIUMPH IN HIS STUBBORN DIGGING!

Chain of Command.

The immediate superior of the Leader of a Rescue Squad is known as the Chief of Rescue Service. He has the following duties to perform:

Administrative.—Including enrollment, discipline, maintenance, organization, and efficiency of the men for that part of the Rescue Service of which he is in charge.

Training.—Including preparation, execution, and general supervision of a program of training in rescue work for those men over whom he is in charge.

Operational.—Including activities of Rescue Squad personnel during air raids.

The Chief of Rescue Service or one of his assistants will direct the Leader in accordance with these three basic duties. The Leader, in turn, will direct the Rescue Squad in accordance with the orders of the Chief of Rescue Service. The Leader has a high sense of responsibility to the Chief of Rescue Service on the one hand and to members of the Rescue Squad on the other.

The Rescue Squad.—The Rescue Squad of which the Leader is in charge will consist of 10 men and a driver. If possible, the 10 men should be proportioned as follows:

1. Former coal or hard-rock miner (if possible, one trained in rescue work by the Bureau of Mines).
2. House wrecker.
3. Scaffolder.
4. Structural-steel erector.
5. Plumber.
6. Electrician.

7. Handyman.
8. Handyman.
9. Helper.
10. Helper.

Since a new problem will confront the Rescue Squad each time it operates, it is probable that rescue procedure will not be exactly the same in any two cases. Therefore, in choosing personnel, emphasis must be placed on inherent capacity and resourcefulness. Every effort must be made to obtain men skilled in handling mechanized equipment and familiar with house-wrecking work. Providing some of the Rescue Squad personnel are so qualified, then the primary need is for *unskilled* assistance—men who have the physical endurance and the will to perform the arduous duties which rescue work involves— men who have physical qualifications which permit heavy and hard work for long hours, possibly under the encumbrance of a gas mask or an oxygen-breathing apparatus, or in an atmosphere low in oxygen or containing varying amounts of combustible or toxic gases. About 25,000 men in various parts of the country have been trained by the United States Bureau of Mines in mine-rescue work. Wherever possible, the services of such trained personnel should be enlisted in organization of the Rescue Service for civil protection.

The Leader.—The Leader of a Rescue Squad holds a position of special responsibility and trust, demanding exceptional qualities of reliability and perseverance. Perseverance, beginning with the Leader and emanating to all members of the Squad, will overcome the set-backs, difficulties, and long hours of seemingly useless "digging" into tons of rubble and debris which usually precede the rescue of those buried alive.

Since human lives are at stake, the Leader of the Rescue Squad must never fail in his responsibility. As *he* is reliable, so will his men be. To this end, he must be methodical, make thoughtful preparation for his work, carry it out in orderly sequence, and keep a careful record of what is done. Above all, he must be clear in his own mind as to what he wants done, how he wants it done, and why he wants it done.

The Driver.—The Leader of a Rescue Squad should understand the relationship of the Driver to the Chief of Rescue Service. The Driver is responsible to the Chief for the condition and running of the Rescue Squad truck and its readiness to take the road at any time during the night or day. Immediately after he has reported for duty the incoming Driver should satisfy himself by personal inspection that the vehicle is in good running order. Any loss, damage, defect, or repair, or adjustment of major importance, both of the vehicle and of tools, should be reported to the Chief of Rescue Service for such further action as may be necessary.

The Rescue Squad Depot.—Rescue Squads are organized in depots which house members of the squad and their transport. On the average, only one Rescue Squad will be housed in each Depot and there will be one Depot for every 25,000 people. The place selected as a depot should be protected against air raids as much as possible.

Training.—Instruction in special duties of Rescue Squads will be given at the Rescue Squad Depots where lectures, training, and practice in this connection will be carried out.

Rescue Squad

EQUIPMENT

Rescue work is usually carried on under the direction of the Fire Department, and the basis of the equipment in each instance will be whatever the individual department can supply. A list of equipment, comprehensive and reasonably adequate for most emergencies, is authorized for each Rescue Squad with the aim that it shall be met as nearly as possible by each group.

Some incidents of a major character will necessitate swift removal of massive lumps of brickwork and masonry, dragging away of masses of tangled trusses, girders, and other debris, rapid cutting up of portions of reinforced concrete and their removal to facilitate rescue and generally to make access. For this purpose it is desirable that the Chief of Rescue Service should contact the contractors, works managers, filling-station operators, and garages in their area and compile a record of such heavy equipment as lifting gear, portable derricks, winches, gasoline-driven equipment, mechanical excavators, lengths of heavy chain, and other heavy gear which might be useful in an emergency.

Care of Equipment.—Rescue Squads are expected to look after their equipment, to keep it clean and in working order, to watch for wear, tear, and defects, and to report them at once and to account for any loss.

Each Squad should be in possession of a list of the equipment with which it has been furnished, and it is recommended that this list be mounted on a board and kept on the truck. The list should be produced and used as a basis for checking the equipment at each change of shift, at equipment inspections and after incidents.

The whole Squad is responsible for the equipment in the truck, but where the Squad is in action at an exercise or an incident, the Driver, by reason of his duty to stand by the truck, should act as the Squad's storekeeper at such times, and check each item of equipment returned to the truck against that issued. The importance of such a careful check cannot be emphasized too greatly. Equipment is costly and replaced with difficulty. Since additional air raids may occur before a lost item can be replaced, it is important that each Squad member feel a personal responsibility for seeing that items of equipment are returned to the Driver.

Trucks.—Type: Rescue Squads are equipped with open and covered trucks. Each has particular advantages and disadvantages related to the uses to which it may be put, and for this reason, wherever possible both types should be on hand at each depot.

The covered truck offers best protection to the contents and the greater area of interior surface lends itself readily to the storage of articles of equipment. A truck with a canvas top is especially desirable. The open truck can be used for removing and for carrying debris or special equipment. However, in this case, it must be fitted up in a manner that enables it to be unloaded easily and the floor to be cleared completely and quickly.

Planning the Truck Unit.—Much technical skill is needed in planning an efficient system of storage in a truck. Principal rules are:

1. Provide a clear floor space. It is wrong and unnecessary for men to have to stand on their equipment when manning the truck.

2. Group the equipment. One of the most difficult items to store is the protective clothing, and the planning of this is often the key to the planning of the rest of the equipment.

3. Let instant accessibility of each item form the basis of the detailed planning.

Caution: Heavy items must be adequately secured or rested on the floor of the truck. Serious accidents have occurred to the personnel when jacks, for example, have become unfastened during a journey.

The Trailer.—The primary object of a trailer is to provide a means of carrying equipment to places where it may be impossible or undesirable to take the truck.

List of Equipment.—Following is a schedule of equipment authorized for a Rescue Squad of 10:

Personal Equipment, per man (Recommended):
   1 Steel helmet.
   1 Civilian duty gas mask (when available).
   1 Heavy water-resistant suit of jacket and trousers.
   1 Pair (leather) heavy work gloves.

1 Pair canvas work gloves.

1 Pair rubber boots.

1 Pair heavy leather lace boots.

1 Waterproof coat.

Rescue Equipment, per squad (Recommended):

A supply of timber.

3 20-ft. scaffold poles.

2 Iron-shod levers (10 ft. or 12 ft.).

2 Small acetylene lamps; a tin of carbide; a can of water.

1 Heavy axe.

6 Firemen's axes.

1 Set of rope tackle (a 3-sheave, a 2-sheave, and a 100-ft. 3-in. rope).

1 200-ft. length Manila or Sisal rope (3 in.).

7 40-ft. lengths 1½-in. Manila lashing lines (including one for stretcher sling)

1 100-ft. length ⅝-in. wire rope with thimbles and shackle.

2 50-ft. lengths ⅝-in. wire rope with thimbles and shackle.

1 chain lifting tackle.

1 6-ft. chain (3-ton lift).

1 6-ft. chain (2-ton lift).

2 6-ft. chains (1½-ton lift).

1 Single sheave snatch block.

1 Pulley wheel and basket sling.

1 Set of chain tackle.

2 Jacks with 10- or 15-ton lift.

1 35-ft. ladder (extension).

10 Small electric hand lamps.

4 Large electric hand lamps.

1 Portable electric light and cable connections.

2 Pairs rubber gloves (for handling electric cables).

9

5 Pairs rubber gloves for postmortem work.

1 Two-handled cross-cut saw.

6 15-ft. lengths of 1¼-in. wire rope.

1 100-ft. length ⅝-in. wire rope with thimbles and shackle.

1 50-ft. length ⅝-in. wire rope with thimbles and shackle.

6 Picks (light, 4 lb.), or cross mattocks.

3 Crowbars.

9 Pointed shovels or forks.

3 Sledge hammers.

2 Hand saws.

2 Wheelbarrows.

4 Hurricane lamps.

6 Debris baskets.

2 Bucket pumps (for combating incendiaries).

1 Tarpaulin or sheets of corrugated iron (to protect trapped persons from falling debris until released).

*Box of miscellaneous tools, spikes, timber dogs, etc.

Timber, blocks for fulcrums for levers, folding wedges, etc.

Supply of puddled clay, for dealing with gas leaks.

*Contents of the Box of Tools:

1 Claw hammer (size 5).

1 Pincers, 8 in.

1 Wooden mallet.

1 12-in. hacksaw frame and blade, with 12 spare blades.

1 Marking gauge.

3 Cold chisels, 8-in., 12-in., and 18-in. by ¾-in.

1 Pair 12-in. steel wedges, with tongs.

1 Square, 10½-in.

1 Stilson wrench, 14 in.
2 Double-hooped wood chisels, 1-in. and ¾-in.
1 Short two-edged pruning saw.
1 Club hammer, 3 lb.
1 Brace with ¾-in. and 1-in. center bits.
1 Flooring awl.
1 Bolt cutter.
1 Wheel-type pipe cutter.
1 Scaffolder's hammer.
1 Stopcock key.

First-Aid Equipment:

1 First-Aid box.
2 First-Aid pouches.

Action of Rescue Party

AT AIR RAID INCIDENT

Upon Receipt of an Alert:

1. On the receipt of a yellow warning message, the Rescue Squad should go immediately to its depot and should remain there until further instructions are received. The Driver should satisfy himself that the engine of his truck will start and should then join the rest of the Squad in the shelter.

2. The Leader with his messenger should wait for telephone instructions from the responsible Chief of Rescue Service. On receipt of instructions dispatching his Squad to an incident the Leader should send his messenger to instruct the Squad to prepare for action.

3. The Leader should inspect the men to see that they are properly equipped. They should be

wearing steel helmets and have gas masks. Two of the men should be equipped with water bottles, another should carry blankets. One of the men with water bottles should also carry first-aid box and splints. Another should be equipped with fireman's ax and torch. The Leader should also carry a torch.

Transit to the Scene of an Incident.— *The Route:* The Squad should proceed to the incident following any special route or direction relayed by the Depot Superintendent from the control center, and the Driver should follow the instructions given by the Leader *en route.* If obstruction is met with on the way, an alternative means of access to the incident should be sought and the obstruction reported to the control center.

Traffic Lights.—Drivers should obey automatic traffic signals even when on urgent duty during an air raid, unless they can see with certainty that the road is absolutely clear. It must be remembered that other vehicles on errands of equal urgency may be traveling the same road.

Approach to Contaminated Areas.— When gas is present, the direction of the wind should be noted and the Squad should avoid approaching the scene of the incident in the face of a wind that is tainted with gas. In such a case the Driver should make sufficient detour to arrive "with the wind" and take especial care not to drive into a contaminated area and thus expose his vehicle and its equipment to the risk of contamination. He should approach the scene of the incident slowly in order to establish contact with guides, wardens, or "Incident Officers."

Incident Officer.—Where the circumstances at an incident necessitate it, the Commander will send an Incident Officer to represent him on the spot for the purpose of coordinating the work of the services. For this purpose he will establish a *Reporting Base* at which all available information will be centralized and from which general supervision will be exercised over the progress and conduct of the incident.

He should not supervise the technique of rescue and first-aid work, but he should look to the Squad Leaders to cooperate with each other under his general direction and to keep him informed as to the progress of the work.

The Incident Officer, who is responsible for seeing that Squads are summoned in sufficient strength, should form a link between the incident and the Commander (keeping the latter informed as to progress of events), and should act as an agent for the respective services whereby reinforcements of personnel, materials, and equipment can be obtained when request is made to him.

Arrival at Scene of Incident.—*Immediate Action:* On arrival at the scene of an incident, the Leader should halt the vehicle in a reasonable position relative to the incident, taking care not to block other traffic and should act on any directions which may be given by Auxiliary Police, or Wardens instructed to direct traffic. The Leader, accompanied by his messenger, should report to the Incident Officer in charge at the control post or reporting base or to the senior officer present. He should give the place of origin of his Squad and its number, and request instructions.

13

The Squad should remain on the truck until it is parked. The trailer should be unhooked and withdrawn about 8 feet to the most advantageous position or the parking place.

Reporting.—When reporting to the Incident Officer or to the senior officer present the Leader should obtain from him whatever information can be supplied and confirm by his own observations:

(a) The extent and nature of the damage.

(b) Whether gas is present and the type (persistent or nonpersistent).

(c) Where persons are trapped and the approximate number.

(d) The presence of collapsed or dangerous floors and walls.

(e) Whether gas, water, or electric supplies have been damaged and require immediate attention in the interests of the casualties.

He should advise the Incident Officer immediately of any serious dangers discovered by him which require immediate or special attention, and of any requests which he may have in respect to rescue operations or the parking of his vehicle.

Procedure of Rescue.—*Preliminary Survey:* Having been allocated his portion of the work, the Leader should make a swift preliminary survey and such interim arrangements as will enable the Squad to concentrate on the most urgent matters while he completes the reconnaissance in detail and until he has formulated his organization for dealing with the work as a whole. If the case is beyond the resources of the Squads present, he should inform the Incident Officer immediately and request the summoning of further Rescue Squads.

Priority.—Questions may arise as to the precedence of services at an incident and any point of this nature should be settled by the Incident Officer or the senior ranking officer present. It is generally agreed, however, that when rescue work is urgent, it should take precedence of all services except the Fire Service. Rescue Leaders should make contact with each other, and actively collaborate among themselves and with Leaders of other services.

Where No Incident Officer Is Available.—When no Incident Officer is available, the initial responsibility for representing the Rescue Service and for preliminary reconnaissance and organization of rescue work should lie with the first Leader on the scene. He should likewise set up a distinguishable reporting base and keep it manned by one of his men when he is absent from it. Any other Leader arriving subsequently should cooperate faithfully under his collective leadership, and the first Leader should be prepared to continue directing in this capacity until he is relieved by a senior officer of the Service, even if he should find that the work may extend beyond the boundary of his own area into that of another.

Reconnaissance.—If a building has not been demolished, systematic search, beginning at the lowest floor level should be made for trapped victims. Search should not be abandoned until all parts of the building and debris have been thoroughly examined, and a search of adjacent buildings made. The position and condition of the casualties should be carefully noted and recorded and the information passed on to the Stretcher Teams and Wardens at the earliest moment. The Leader should carry a pencil and notebook and should be prepared to make a brief sketch or block plan showing where the more serious damage is located, where casualties are known to await rescue and, if collective rescue work is being carried on, where the various Rescue Squads have been set to work.

Before decision is made as to which of the badly injured victims should be rescued first, the nature of the injuries, position of the victim, and work involved in rescue should all be considered. When a casualty is located and injuries ascertained, it is desirable that a label be attached stating when the casualty was found. This procedure will be of value in case the casualty subsequently dies unidentified.

Method of Locating Victims.—A system of tapping such as that employed in mines should be adopted. Tapping can be done readily on a pipe, beam, or solid structure extending into the debris. A system of signals is not necessary. If taps are measured, the buried person will reply in kind providing he is still conscious.

The Work of Rescue.—Having satisfied himself as to the number, location, and types of casualties, the Leader should direct his men on the work of rescue. Necessary operations should be carried out with great care so that dangerous movement of debris will not result.

16

The Rescue Squad may be expected to move injured persons from the upper floors, basements, over obstacles and rough ground, and to make every effort to get them where they will receive attention or be taken to the first-aid post or hospital. If available, the First-Aid Party is responsible for the casualty when the Rescue Squad Leader decides that no further danger will be encountered in removal; and Rescue Squads should not normally move a casualty further than is necessary to remove any possibility of additional injury. If First-Aid Parties are not present, the Rescue Squad will naturally give emergency first aid to the injured.

Rescue Procedure.—Each case of rescue work will differ from every other and, for this reason, no set of rules as to procedure can be laid down. It may be necessary to sink a small shaft vertically downward into a mound of debris, and to lower a man into the shaft, thus permitting him to worm his body round to a position where he may best be able to speak with the buried people and more certainly determine their location.

Work with the hands is often the only possible way of dealing with the "rubble" which is left from an air raid. In making a tunnel sufficiently large to permit a man to crawl through, the best procedure is to fill small baskets with bits of debris and pass them from hand to hand to the mouth of the tunnel where they can be emptied.

Dangerous Buildings.—During rescue operations, shoring and demolition should be done only where it is essential for the safety of rescuers and casualties. Wrecked buildings must be entered cautiously, and in walking across damaged floors, rescue workers should stay as close as possible to the wall, noting which way floor joists run, and using the supported end of the joists to avoid undue strain.

Men should consider the probable consequence of every move they propose to make and, although the greatest speed possible is essential, the desire to release victims should not over-balance sound principles of procedure.

Parts of a building which are in a state highly dangerous to the public or are impeding rescue operations should be removed or secured, but attention should be given to possible effects of moving debris which is supporting any part of the structure.

Demolished Buildings.—*Methods of Approach:* When effecting rescue from the wreckage of demolished buildings, early decision should be made as to whether to work down from the top of the debris or to tunnel beneath it. The choice between, or in certain circumstances, the combination of these two methods, will depend upon the conditions at the scene of the incident, and upon reliable information as to the probable location of the occupants which may be given by Air-Raid Wardens, Incident Officer, police, neighbors, or persons who have escaped or been rescued from the building.

In directing the work of his men, the Leader will need to utilize his knowledge of planning, construction, and materials to the utmost in the interests of speed and safety. Advantage should be taken of every wall or opening that is likely to afford some degree of security for exploring the wreckage, and to provide an avenue of approach to the trapped persons. Men should be posted to watch all dangerous structures that are likely to collapse and injure those working. Care should be taken to avoid landslides and further injury to the victims. Save where otherwise practicable all debris in the vicinity of the trapped will have to be moved by hand, and should be deposited clear of the·site of rescue in order to avoid the possibility of burying other victims.

Tunnelling and Stripping Debris.— When the trapped are understood to be in the lower part of the building—and this is likely to be most often the case—*tunneling* generally provides the swiftest means of access. The other alternative is *stripping the site of debris*. Both methods require the greatest care. Location of victims is very often a matter of reasoned guesswork upon the accuracy of which the chances of survival of the victims depend. The principle of using the recognizable remaining elements of the structure as a basis from which to start the search should be adopted.

No movement should be allowed on top of debris beneath which men are tunnelling. Tunnellers should wear helmets, and handkerchiefs over their noses and mouths. They should be attached by a line before entering under dangerous wreckage, and men should be posted, and arrangements made, to give them any assistance, to pass back messages and to provide them with any article of equipment which they may require. There should be no crowding, confusion, or unauthorized talking or shouting, and a strict watch should be kept for any movement or sound coming from the debris.

Fire and Water.—The turning off of the gas, water, and electricity mains should receive prompt attention. The Fire Service should be summoned when basements are flooded and when rescue operations must be carried on from excessive heights inaccessible to the Rescue Squads with the equipment at their disposal. A powerful electric handlamp should be used in buildings to assist the search for casualties when gas mains and service pipes have been damaged.

Shoring and Demolition.—Rescue Squads should confine themselves, as regards shoring up, demolition and repair, to tasks of immediate urgency and limited scope. The Leader should inform the Incident Officer of any portions of the building which are likely to collapse and endanger life so that the Demolition and Clearance Crews can be called to deal with them.

Completion of Work.— Upon completion of the work on the site, the Leader should see that equipment is collected and checked, line up his men, call the roll, make a verbal report of the work carried out to the Incident Officer, and await instructions as to further work or as to the Squad's return to the Depot. It should be re-emphasized that the Squad should not leave the scene until all equipment is accounted for since loss of one item may make subsequent rescue impossible. On returning to the Depot, members of the Squad should proceed at once to render themselves, their equipment, and their truck ready for further duty if called upon.

Recurring Raids.—If another air attack occurs while the Squad is traveling to or from an incident, the Leader should take all necessary steps to protect his Squad from becoming casualties, and notify the Control Center as to action taken and his whereabouts if he is delayed.

In the event of a further raid at the scene of an incident, men should take care not to be unduly exposed and should see that casualties are quickly sheltered. At night, flares should be extinguished, or the source of light concealed.

Leader's Report.—The Leader should record the numbers of injured and dead that have been removed from the buildings and their identification if possible, the address of the property where they were found, the quantity of shoring used, and the loss of any equipment and report these on his return to the Depot.

LEADER'S REPORT FORM

Squad No. _____ Address of depot _____ Date _____
Scene of work _____
Nature of work _____
Work done _____
_____ Was work completed? _____
Number of injured removed _____
Number of dead removed _____
Particulars of materials and equipment used, lost, or
   damaged _____

_____

_____
Number of men in squad _____ Hours worked _____
Casualties to personnel _____
Name of leader _____
   Further information and full particulars of persons
rescued on other side of form.

In addition, a careful record should be kept of the operations in order that the Leader may be able to hand over to the relieving Leader and his relief shift the history of the incident. Unnecessary duplication of work may thus be prevented.

Salvage of Private Property.—The primary responsibility for recovering and protecting removable goods from a damaged building rests with the owner, and subject to the requirements of the civilian protection services engaged at the scene of the damage; facilities should be afforded to owners to recover their possessions. The *Municipal Authorities* should endeavor to give such assistance as may be required for the removal and local transport of goods or articles, their storage, and their protection against loss or further damage, particularly where persons are rendered homeless.

Unexploded Bombs.

Members of a Rescue Squad should not attempt to remove unexploded bombs. The Leader should notify the police of the location of the bomb, rope off the danger area in the vicinity, and suspend further work in that area until the bomb is removed or exploded.

Gas-Proof Clothing.

The following procedure in regard to gas-proof clothing should be carried out by Rescue Squads:

1. If gas has been reported when a Rescue Squad is called out, members of the Squad should put on protective clothing before leaving the Depot.

2. If gas has not been reported, members of the Squad should not put on protective clothing, but should take it with them in case gas is found to be present or to be used by the enemy at a later stage of the attack.

3. If it is necessary to put on protective clothing before leaving the Depot, personnel should leave all items of personal clothing except underwear at the Depot in charge of the Depot Leader. Personal clothing and personal effects, including money, should not be taken on the truck.

4. When a Rescue Squad proceeds to an incident where gas has not been reported but where gas is discovered in the interval, personnel should change into protective clothing in an evacuated house or building adjacent to the contaminated area and should then proceed to the incident leaving their personal clothing behind in the building in which change was made.

Incendiary-Bomb Control.

Rescue Squads should not deal with incendiary bombs if personnel adequate to handle them is present. However, there may be occasions when it is necessary for members of the Rescue Service to assist with small fires at the scene of rescue work.

The main point of concern in this connection will be with small fires caused by incendiary bombs dropped among the wreckage of a demolished or partly demolished building. If persons are trapped, certain rescue work may have to be postponed until the fire is under control.

If incendiary bombs require attention, the Leader should detail certain members of the Rescue Squad to deal with them. Because of debris considerable difficulty may be experienced in approaching the source of such a fire. Men should approach as near to the fire as possible, lying down or keeping low with their faces near the floor. In this position it will be found easier to breathe and to see. In their approach to the bombs men should have axes handy for dealing with obstacles.

When the fire is under control and the bomb is entirely consumed, there is still a danger that fire may have crept into unseen places where it may remain unnoticed for some time in a smoldering condition. A thorough search should be made for this purpose and it may be necessary to lift floor boards or to remove paneling and skirting from walls if concealed smoldering is suspected.

BLACKOUTS

Blackouts are ordered only on the authority of the War Department. A blackout may be ordered during any period when hostile forces are believed to be in the vicinity, whether or not enemy airplanes have been sighted.

"Blacking Out" a city means that light sources must be so hidden or dimmed that an enemy bomber will have difficulty in finding the target and lack aiming points such as main street intersections. Following are the general plans used.

Street Lights. These are fitted with low-watt bulbs and covers that diffuse the light.

Automobiles. Headlights must be covered except for a small pair of slits and hooded.

Traffic Lights. Are treated the same way as automobile headlights.

Buildings. Windows and doors must be covered with opaque materials. Paint on the glass, heavy curtains, light "baffles" or screens are some of the ways. No cracks of light must show.

Aids to Seeing. Since people have to move about during a blackout, the lack of light may be somewhat offset and safety promoted by—

1. Painting curbs, trees, poles and hydrants with white paint. There is a luminous paint, also, that gives off a faint blue light quite visible in total darkness.

2. Painting signs of luminous paint or making them of fluorescent material on which shines ultraviolet or "black" light or installing dimly lighted signs with horizontal screens to diffuse the light.

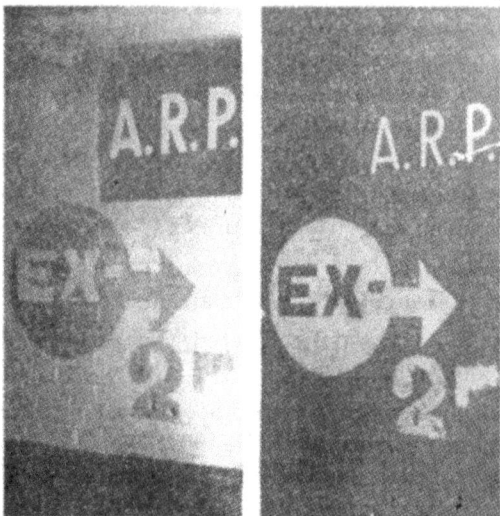

3. Painting white fenders and stripes around automobiles.

Members of the Citizens' Defense Corps who have outside duties during a blackout can be identified more easily if they wear a white cap or white-painted helmet; also a white belt fitted with crossed straps over the shoulders.

Individual Conduct During a Blackout.

Observe traffic rules. Keep to the right and remember the man or vehicle approaching *from* your right *has* the right of way.

If you must smoke, go into a hallway or covered place to strike the match. No smoking in the open is an even better rule. Make all crossings at intersections. It is hard for a driver to see you.

Be sure that everyone you know is acquainted with these simple rules.

DO NOT run when air raid warnings sound after dark during blackouts.

Use your flashlight as little as possible, if at all. Never point it upward.

Curb edges and direction signs painted white will help you find your way.

Keep pets on leash if you take them out after dark.

If an air raid warning sounds, get under cover, you may be hit by shell fragments.

If you don't know the neighborhood the first policeman or warden will tell you where to go.

ARMY

1

When an observer sights a group of hostile planes, he picks up his telephone (1) and says *Army Flash*. The Central Operator (2) at once connects him with the assigned Filter Center (3) to which he reports the type of planes, number, height, and direction of flight. When several reports agree, watchers transmit the data to an Information Center (4) where developments over a large area are plotted on a huge map.

Watching the map, Air Corps officers order interceptor planes into the air, (5) direct them to contact with the enemy; another officer notes the cities threatened and flashes a yellow, blue, or red alarm, according to the degree of danger, to the proper Warning District Center (6).

At this point, Civilian Defense takes over from the Air Corps, telephones the warnings to Control Centers (7) within the Warning District. And here the Commander of the local Citizens' Defense Corps orders the alert, has the public warning sounded usually short blasts on air horns, power horns or steam whistles or on the wailing sirens—and if the bombers arrive overhead, directs the operation of passive defense. Learn the air raid warning for your city.

FLASH

2

3

4

5

6

7

The Refuge Room

WHAT TO DO IN AN AIR RAID

At the yellow warning, if you are not already on duty, you will be summoned to your post and will carry out orders until relieved. However, here are the rules for those who do not have assigned duties when the air raid warning comes. Memorize them carefully so that you can in turn instruct others. Here is what to tell them:

1. If away from home, seek the nearest shelter. Get off the street.

2. If you are driving, first park your car at the curb; be sure all lights are shut off.

3. If you are at home, send the others to the refuge room. This should be a comfortable place with as little window exposure as possible, equipped with drinking water, things to read, toilet facilities, a flashlight, a portable radio, a sturdy table, and food if you like.

4. Turn off all gas stove burners but leave pilot lights, water heaters and furnaces alone. Leave electricity and water on. Fill some large containers or a bathtub with water.

5. Check up on blackout arrangements. Don't let a crack of light show to the outside.

6. See that everyone's eyeglasses and dentures are in the refuge room. There should be additional warm garments for everyone, too.

7. Keep out of line of windows. Fragments and glass splinters cause most casualties.

8. If bombs fall nearby, get under a heavy table, an overturned davenport.

9. Don't rush out when the "all clear" signal sounds. Maintain the blackout. The Raiders may return.

10. Otherwise, keep cool; be sensible and set an example to others.

FIRE DEFENSE

IT WILL BE VERY DIFFICULT TO FIGHT A MAGNESIUM BOMB UNLESS SOME WORK IS DONE BEFORE THE ATTACK

ALL FURNITURE TRUNKS AND JUNK OF ALL KINDS SHOULD BE REMOVED FROM ATTIC OR TOP FLOOR!

ROOF BEAMS JOISTS AND STUDS CAN BE TREATED TO RESIST FLAME — GIVING MORE TIME TO REACH THE BOMB

PAINT DOES NO GOOD! A HEAVY COAT OF ORDINARY WHITEWASH HELPS SOME

HOW THE MAGNESIUM BOMB WORKS

THE MOST EFFECTIVE INCENDIARY BOMB MADE SO FAR IS THE **MAGNESIUM BOMB**

FINS OR VANES TO GUIDE FALL

CASING OF MAGNESIUM A LIGHT WEIGHT METAL SIMILAR TO ALUMINUM

ESCAPE HOLES

STRIKING HEAD

LENGTH, ABOUT 14" WEIGHT, 2.2 POUNDS

A LARGE BOMBER CAN CARRY 1000 SUCH BOMBS!

THEY ARE USUALLY RELEASED 20 TO 50 AT A TIME, SPREAD LIKE SHOT BEFORE STRIKING.

DROPPED FROM A HEIGHT OF 20,000 FEET, THEY DEVELOP ENOUGH FORCE TO PENETRATE AN AVERAGE ROOF...

...THUS, THEY USUALLY START BURNING IN A TOP STORY OR ATTIC

THE THERMITE FILLING OF IRON OXIDE AND FINELY DIVIDED ALUMINUM IS THEN IGNITED AND DEVELOPS A FIERCE HEAT OF **OVER 4500 DEGREES!**

THE FLAME ROARS OUT OF THE ESCAPE HOLES.

THE MAGNESIUM CASING CATCHES FIRE, WITH A SPUTTERING ACTION...

...FLAMING MOLTEN METAL IS THROWN ABOUT AND SURROUNDING INFLAMMABLE MATERIAL CATCHES FIRE

IF NOT QUICKLY QUENCHED, THE BOMB WILL BURN THROUGH THE FLOOR, SETTING ADDITIONAL FIRES ON THE FLOOR BELOW...

BUT, WITH PROMPT ACTION AND SIMPLE TOOLS, A MAGNESIUM BOMB CAN BE QUENCHED!

CONTROLLING WITH WATER

To FIGHT A BOMB WITH WATER, YOU NEED TWO MEN AND SPECIAL EQUIPMENT. REMEMBER, YOU CAN'T PUT OUT THE BOMB — YOU FEED IT WATER, TO BURN OUT!

ONE MAN PUMPS 80 STROKES A MINUTE TO KEEP A STRONG ENOUGH PRESSURE TO THROW A JET 30 FEET, AS SPRAY, 15 FEET. ONE MAN FIGHTS THE FIRE.

JET ON SURROUNDINGS!

YOU USE UP A BUCKET IN 1½ MINUTES

SPECIAL DOUBLE ACTION PUMP WITH 30 FEET OF HOSE AND SPECIAL NOZZLE NEEDED.

SPRAY ON BOMB

A THIRD PERSON IS MOST USEFUL TO CHECK OTHER POINTS FOR FLAME REPLENISH WATER AND RELIEVE PUMPER.

AMPLE STORAGE OF WATER SHOULD BE PROVIDED IN ADVANCE, AS WATER MAINS MAY BE BROKEN BY HIGH EXPLOSIVES AND PRESSURE LOST! FILL THE TUB, EXTRA PAILS AND DON'T FORGET IN A PINCH — THE CONTENTS OF HOT WATER OR HEATING BOILERS!

NEVER THROW THE CONTENTS OF A WATER PAIL ON A BOMB!

...IT WILL SCATTER WITH EXPLOSIVE VIOLENCE!

IF CONTROL OF THE BOMB SEEMS DOUBTFUL, HAVE AN ALARM TURNED IN, BUT CONTINUE FIGHTING THE BOMB UNTIL HELP ARRIVES OR SUPPLIES ARE EXHAUSTED!

1 LEARN NOW HOW TO CALL

2 LEARN NOW LOCATION OF NEAREST ALARM...

MILTON CANIFF

CONTROLLING WITH SAND

APPROACH THE BOMB IN A CROUCHING OR CRAWLING POSITION. PLACE THE SAND BUCKET, UPSET, TO ALLOW A FULL-ARM SWING TOWARD THE BOMB

TRY TO COVER THE BOMB WITH DRY SAND, TO CONFINE IT'S ACTION, SO THAT YOU CAN GET NEAR ENOUGH TO SCOOP IT UP ON THE SHOVEL

WHEN THE BOMB IS UNDER FAIR CONTROL, SCOOP IT UP ON THE SHOVEL, FIRST RIGHTING THE BUCKET, BUT LEAVING SOME SAND IN THE BOTTOM...

... IF THE BOMB CAN BE DROPPED FROM A WINDOW TO SOME PLACE WHERE IT CAN BURN OUT WITHOUT HARM —

GET RID OF IT THAT WAY!

... OTHERWISE, PUT IT IN THE BUCKET ON TOP OF SAND, COVER IT WITH MORE SAND...

...THEN, HOLDING THE BUCKET ON THE SHOVEL, CARRY IT OUT OF THE HOUSE...

ABOUT FIRE EXTINGUISHERS

Many houses and public buildings have fire extinguishers. They will be as useful as ever in putting out fires caused by an incendiary bomb. For putting out the bomb itself, the extinguisher may not be suitable.

Read the label. If it says that the contents include CARBON TETRACHLORIDE, it cannot under any circumstances be used on a magnesium bomb. It is not only ineffective, it may cause dangerous gas to be generated. After the bomb is burnt out, use it on any remaining fire.

All water-type extinguishers are suitable. If the label says SODA-ACID, that's simply a means of creating pressure in the extinguisher. Turn it upside down, use it. You can get a spray effect by putting the thumb over the nozzle, use the jet on surrounding fires. However, *one extinguisher is not enough to burn out a magnesium bomb*. And you cannot refill the extinguisher.

It is best to have sand or pump-bucket equipment handy, use them on the bomb, and save the extinguishers for resulting fires.

A foam extinguisher will also help to control a bomb, but one extinguisher load will not finish the job.

See that the extinguishers you know about are ready for use.

CHEMICAL WARFARE AGENTS
REFERENCE AND TRAINING CHART

LEGEND

HOSPITAL CASE	FIRST AID STATION	LUNG PROTECTION NEEDED	COMPLETE PROTECTION NEEDED

The importance of proper first aid for gas victims cannot be overemphasized. The following are general rules which apply in all cases.

A. Act promptly and quietly; be calm.

B. Put a gas mask on the patient if gas is still present or, if he has a mask on, check to see that his is properly adjusted. If a mask is not available, wet a handkerchief or other cloth and have him breathe through it.

C. Keep the patient at absolute rest; loosen clothing to facilitate breathing.

D. Remove the patient to a gas-free place as soon as possible.

E. Summon medical aid promptly; if possible, send the victim to a hospital.

F. Do not permit the patient to smoke, as this causes coughing and, hence, exertion.

CLASS	NAMES AND SYMBOLS	FORM	ODOR	PERSISTENCE	TACTICAL CLASS	PROTECTION	FIRST AID (After removal from gassed area)	PHYSIOLOGICAL EFFECT
VESICANTS	MUSTARD $S(CH_2CH_2)_2Cl_2$ DICHLORETHYL SULFIDE	LIQUID AND VAPOR	Garlic, Horseradish, Mustard	One day to one week. Longer if dry or cold.			Undress; remove liquid mustard with protective ointment, bleach paste, or kerosene; bathe; wash eyes and nose with soda solution.	Delayed effect. Burns skin or membrane. Inflammation respiratory tract leading to pneumonia. Eye irritation, conjunctivitis.
VESICANTS	LEWISITE $CHClCH\text{-}AsCl_2$ CHLORVINYL-DICHLORARSINE	LIQUID AND VAPOR	Geranium	One day to one week. Longer if dry or cold.			Undress; remove liquid Lewisite with hydrogen peroxide, lye in glycerine, or kerosene; bathe; wash eyes and nose with soda. Rest—Doctor.	Burning or irritation of eyes, nasal passages, respiratory tract, skin. Arsenical poison.
LUNG IRRITANTS	CHLORPICRIN CCl_3NO_2 NITROCHLOROFORM	GAS	Flypaper, Anise	Open 6 hours. Woods 12 hours.			Wash eyes, keep quiet and warm. Do not use bandages.	Causes severe coughing, crying, vomiting.
LUNG IRRITANTS	DIPHOSGENE $ClCOOC\text{-}Cl_3$ TRICHLORMETHYL CHLORFORMATE	GAS	Cuttings, Acid	30 minutes.			Keep quiet and warm. Give coffee as a stimulant.	Causes coughing, breathing hurts, eyes water, faint.
LUNG IRRITANTS	PHOSGENE $COCl_2$ CARBONYL CHLORIDE	GAS	Musty hay, Green corn	10 to 20 minutes.			Keep quiet and warm, bed rest. Coffee as a stimulant. Loosen clothing. No alcohol or cigarettes.	Irritation of lungs, occasional vomiting, tears in eyes, dazed feeling. Occasionally symptoms delayed. Later, collapse, heart failure.
LACRIMATORS	CHLORACETOPHENONE $C_6H_5CO\text{-}CH_2Cl$	GAS	Apple Blossoms	10 minutes.			Wash eyes with cold water or boric acid solution. Do not bandage. Face wind. For skin, sodium sulphite solution.	Makes eyes smart. Shut tightly. Tears flow. Temporary.
LACRIMATORS	BROMBENZYLCYANIDE $C_6H_5CH\text{-}BrCN$	GAS	Sour fruit	Several days. (Weeks in winter.)			Wash eyes with boric acid. Do not bandage.	Eyes smart, shut, tears flow. Effect lasts some time. Headache.
STERNUTATORS	ADAMSITE $(C_6H_4)_2\text{-}NHAsCl$ DIPHENYLAMINECHLORARSINE	GAS	Coal Smoke	10 minutes.			Keep quiet and warm. Loosen clothing. Reassure. Spray nose with non-symphine or saltt bleaching powder. Aspirin for headache.	Causes sneezing, sick depressed feeling, headache.
STERNUTATORS	DIPHENYLCHLORARSINE $(C_6H_5)_2\text{-}AsCl$	SMOKE	Shoe Polish	Summer 10 minutes.			Remove to pure air. Keep quiet. Aspirin. Sniff chlorine from bleaching powder bottle.	Causes sick feeling and headache.

36

WAR GASES

General Notes.

War "Gases," or chemical agents used to produce casualties, are surprise weapons. As this is written, they have not been used against the British or others trained to protect themselves. They have been used against the Ethiopians and the Chinese.

A gas-tight room suitably located offers fair protection against any probable concentration of war gas in a city. For those whose duties take them into the streets a gas mask offers full protection against all but the "blister gases" (liquid vesicants). To enter areas where mustard or lewisite is present, full protective clothing is needed.

War gases may be dropped in bombs or simple containers and liquid vesicants may also be sprayed by airplanes.

The gas warning is a "percussion sound"— that is, bells, drums, hand rattles, rapidly struck resonant objects of any kind. If the presence of gas is suspected, report to the nearest warden. Do not shout if distant gas alarms are heard. The danger is local and the spreading of an alarm must be left to the wardens.

The notes on the following pages are simply for reference for those who have received instruction in protection against gas. Reading them will not by itself make you an expert in gas defense.

THE GAS-TIGHT ROOM

War gases hug the ground, flow into cellars and basements. Upper floors of a dwelling are away from dangerous concentrations. If all openings and cracks are closed, a room three stories from the ground will offer good protection against war gases.

To stop cracks and small openings, tape of various kinds may be used. A mush made by soaking newspapers in water or patching plaster may be used for caulking larger openings. A piece of wall board, nails and caulking material may be kept handy to cover a window broken by the blast of high explosives.

One door may be used as an entrance by fastening over it a blanket in such a way as to seal it tightly when no one is going in or out. If soaked in oil to close the air spaces, the blanket is more effective.

Store necessary supplies in such a room—food, water, chairs, a battery-operated radio, flashlight and by all means provide some sort of toilet facilities use it as the refuge room.

Allow 20 square feet of floor space for each person who is to occupy an average room with a ceiling nine feet high. This will give enough air to occupy the room 10 hours.

The illustration shows where to stop up cracks, how to hang the blanket at the entrance door.

"Blister Gases" and Decontamination.

Lewisite and mustard "gas" are liquids in the normal state. They give off a dangerous vapor that acts as a war gas and unless chemically neutralized may persist for a week, contaminating the air for a considerable distance down wind.

Full protection against these chemical agents is afforded by gas-proof clothing, covering the wearer from top to toe and tightened at wrists and ankles. The greatest care must be used in undressing after exposure to lewisite or mustard and this is done at personnel decontamination stations, where vesicant casualties are also taken for first aid.

Decontamination of streets, walls, and buildings is effected principally by means of chloride of lime (bleaching powder) freshly mixed with earth and water as a slurry or paste. It must be thoroughly worked into cracks and crevices and the resulting product flushed away. This work is done by the decontamination squads.

The liquid vesicants are very penetrating and ordinary shoes or clothing offer no protection. Do not go into the streets after a gas alarm has been sounded except on direction of the Warden.

RANK DESIGNATION	▲	▲▲	▲▲▲	△	△△	△△△	★	★★	★★★	★★★★
AIR RAID WARDEN	FIRST CLASS	SENIOR OR SECTOR WARDEN	ZONE LEADER	GROUP LEADER	CHIEF WARDEN	STATE WARDEN	NO OTHER RANKS			
AUXILIARY FIREMEN	"	SQUAD LEADER	PLATOON LEADER	COMPANY LEADER	FIRE CHIEF	STATE FIRE COORDINATOR	NO OTHER RANKS			
AUXILIARY POLICEMEN	"	"	"	"	CHIEF OF POLICE	NO OTHER RANKS				
BOMB SQUADS	"	"	NONE	"	"	NO OTHER RANKS				
RESCUE SQUADS	"	"	DEPOT LEADER	"	FIRE CHIEF	NO OTHER RANKS				
MEDICAL FIELD UNITS	"	TEAM LEADER	SQUAD LEADER	UNIT LEADER	CHIEF OF E.M.S.	STATE MEDICAL DIRECTOR	NO OTHER RANKS			
MEDICAL AUXILIARIES (stretcher teams)	"	" ★	" ★	NO OTHER RANKS						
NURSES' AIDES	NO RANK DESIGNATIONS	NO OTHER DESIGNATIONS								
EMERGENCY FOOD AND HOUSING	FIRST CLASS	UNIT LEADER	DEPOT LEADER	COMPANY LEADER	CHIEF WARDEN	NO OTHER RANKS				
DRIVERS UNITS	"	CONVOY LEADER	"	"	NO OTHER RANKS					
MESSENGERS	"	SENIOR MESSENGER	PLATOON LEADER	"	NO OTHER RANKS					
ROAD REPAIR CREWS	"	CREW LEADER	DEPOT LEADER	"	CHIEF OF EMER. WORK S.					
DEMOLITION AND CLEAR.	"	"	"	"	CHIEF OF EMER. WORK S.	NO OTHER RANKS				
DECONTAMINATION SQUADS	"	SQUAD LEADER	STATION LEADER	"						
FIRE WATCHERS	"	NO OTHER RANKS								
REPAIR CREWS	"	CREW LEADER	SERVICE LEADER	NONE	CHIEF OF UTILITIES	NO OTHER RANKS				
LOCAL STAFF	"	AS REQUIRED		STAFF UNIT LEADER	CONTROLLER	COMMANDER	COORDINATOR	NO OTHER RANKS		
STATE STAFF	"	AS REQUIRED			AS DESIGNATED	AS DESIGNATED	ASST. COORDINATOR	COORDINATOR	NO OTHER RANKS	
U. S. STAFF	"	AS REQUIRED			AS DESIGNATED	AS DESIGNATED	AS DESIGNATED	AS DESIGNATED	REGION DIRECTOR PRINCIPAL ASST'S	U. S. DIRECTOR
EQUIVALENT ARMY TERM	PVT. 1st CLASS	NON-COMM. OFF.	LIEUTENANT	CAPTAIN	MAJOR	COLONEL	BRIG. GEN.	MAJ. GEN.	LIEUT. GEN.	GENERAL

CITIZENS' DEFENSE CORPS

The team of trained civilian services organized to operate the passive defense is known as the Citizens' Defense Corps. It includes regular forces of the city—police, firemen, welfare workers, sanitation men—as well as volunteers. It operates as a unit under the local Defense Coordinator.

Staff.

The Citizens' Defense Corps is headed by a Commander assisted by a staff. His second in command is the Executive Officer. There are others who operate the control center and the communications, account for personnel and property and assign transportation. The Chiefs of the Fire and Police Departments assist him in the passive defense. There is a Chief Air Raid Warden, a Chief of Emergency Medical Services, and others who control groups of the enrolled volunteers. Learn the organization of the Citizens' Defense Corps in your community.

Enrolled Volunteer Services of The Citizens' Defense Corps.

Air Raid Wardens are in complete charge of a sector containing the homes of about 500 people. To them the warden is the embodiment of all Civilian Defense.

Auxiliary Firemen assist the regular fire-fighting forces.

Auxiliary Policemen assist the police department in enforcing blackout restrictions, in traffic control, and in guard duties.

Bomb Squads are specially trained squads of police to handle and dispose of time bombs and duds.

Rescue Squads are trained crews of about 10 men each with special equipment to rescue the injured from debris.

Medical Forces consist of first-aid parties and stretcher squads and personnel at casualty clearing stations. Members of these forces are doctors, trained nurses, and assistants.

Nurses' Aides assist nurses. They have special Red Cross Training.

Emergency Food and Housing Corps members provide welfare services to the needy and homeless.

Drivers Units consist of emergency drivers of vehicles used by the Civilian Defense services.

Messengers carry supplies, dispatches, and messages wherever needed.

Road Repair Crews restore normal flow of traffic as quickly as possible. Utility repair men work with these crews and with demolition squads.

Demolition and Clearance Crews remove rubble, fill bomb craters, and remove unsafe walls or parts of buildings.

Decontamination squad members are specially trained to treat clothing and equipment as well as streets and walls contaminated by war gas.

Fire Watchers must spot and combat incendiary bombs.

A MANUAL OF DRILL
for the
CITIZENS' DEFENSE CORPS

*Adapted from the Basic Field Manual of the
United States Army*

Basic drill is required of a volunteer for award
of the insigne. Drill for units of the Citizens'
Defense Corps, moreover, is recommended as it
helps to coordinate the work of individuals under
a single command. The purposes of drill are:

1 To enable a leader to move his unit from one
place to another in an orderly manner.

2 To aid in disciplinary training by instilling
habits of precision and response to the leader's
orders.

3 To provide a means, through ceremonies, of
enhancing the morale; develop a spirit of cohesion;
and give an interesting spectacle to the public.

4 To give leaders practical training in command-
ing volunteers.

*Drills should be frequent, intensive, and of
short duration.*

General.

A normal squad of volunteers contains 12 men or 12 women, all of one service. It consists of a leader, an assistant leader, and other personnel. As far as practicable, the squad is kept intact. The usual formation of the squad is a single rank or single file. This permits variations in the number of men composing the squad.

To Form the Squad.

The command is; FALL IN. At the command FALL IN the squad forms in line as shown. Squad leader on the squad's extreme right, assistant leader on the squad's extreme left.

To secure uniformity, the tallest leader is put in charge of the first squad, the second tallest in charge of the second squad, etc. Assistant

Fig. I—A Squad in Line

leaders are similarly arranged. Other volunteers are placed according to height beginning with the tallest being placed next to the leader.

On falling in, each man except the one on the left extends his left arm laterally at shoulder height, palm of the hand down, fingers extended and joined. Each man, except the one on the right, turns his head and eyes to the right and places himself in line so that his right shoulder touches lightly the tips of the fingers of the man on his right. As soon as proper intervals have been obtained, each man comes to attention, drops his arm smartly to his side and turns his head to

Fig. II—A Volunteer at Attention

the front, heels are together, feet forming a right angle; knees are straight without stiffness, hips level and drawn back slightly, body erect and resting equally on hips, chest lifted and arched, shoulders square and falling equally. Arms hang straight down without stiffness with the back of the hands out, fingers held naturally. Head erect and squarely to the front, chin drawn in so that the axis of the head and neck is vertical, eyes straight to the front. The weight of the body rests equally on the heels and the balls of the feet. In assuming the position of attention the heels are brought together smartly and audibly.

(Leaders and assistant leaders will be appointed under authority defined by the Chief of the Service of which the squad forms a part.

To Form at Close Intervals.

The commands are: At Close Interval, FALL IN. At the command FALL IN, the volunteers fall in as described above, except that close intervals are obtained by placing the left hands on the hips. In this position the heel of the palm of the hand rests on the hip, the fingers and thumb are extended and joined, and the elbow is in the plane of the body.

Fig. III—A Volunteer Falling in at Close Interval

To Aline the Squad.

If in line, the commands are: Dress Right, DRESS, Ready, Front. At the command DRESS, each man except the one on the left extends his left arm (or if at close interval, places his left hand upon his hip), and all aline themselves to the right. The instructor places himself on the right flank one pace from and in prolongation of the line and facing down the line. From this position he verifies the alinement of the men, ordering individual men to move forward or back as is necessary. Having checked the alinement, he faces to the right in marching and moves three paces forward, halts, faces to the left and commands: Ready, FRONT. At the command FRONT, arms are dropped quietly and smartly to the sides and heads turned to the front.

Rests.

Being at a halt the commands are: FALL OUT, REST, AT EASE, and PARADE REST.

At the command FALL OUT, volunteers leave the ranks but are required to remain in the immediate vicinity.

At the command REST, one foot is kept in place. Silence and immobility are not required.

At the command AT EASE the right foot is

kept in place. Silence but not immobility is required.

At the command of execution REST of Parade REST, move the left foot smartly 12 inches to the left of the right foot keeping the legs straight so that the weight of the body rests equally on both feet. At the same time, clasp the hands behind the back, palms to the rear, thumb and fingers of the right hand clasping the left thumb without constraint; preserving silence and immobility.

Being at any of the rests except FALL OUT, to resume the position of Attention, the commands are Squad (or other unit being commanded) ATTENTION. At the command ATTENTION take that position in your squad.

Eyes right (left).

The commands are: Eyes (Preliminary Command), RIGHT (Command of Execution) (LEFT) Ready FRONT! At the command RIGHT, each man turns his head and eyes to the right. At the command FRONT the head and eyes are turned to the front.

Facings.

(All Facings are executed at the halt.)

To the flank.—The commands are Right (Left) FACE. At the command FACE, slightly raise the left heel and the right toe: Face to the right, turning on the right heel, assisted by a slight pressure on the ball of the left foot. Next, place the left foot beside the right. Exercise Left FACE on the left heel in a corresponding manner.

To the rear.—The commands are: About FACE. At the command FACE, carry the toe of the right foot a half-foot length to the rear and slightly to the left of the left heel without changing

Fig. IV—Executing Right FACE

the position of the left foot; weight of the body mainly on the heel of the left foot; right leg straight without stiffness. (TWO) Face to the rear turning to the right on the left heel and on the ball of the right foot, place the right heel beside the left.

Steps and Marchings.

All steps and marchings executed from the halt, except right step, begin with the left foot.

Quick Time: Being at a halt, to march forward in quick time, the commands are: Forward MARCH. At the command Forward, shift the weight of the body to the right leg without perceptible movement. At the command MARCH, step off smartly with the left foot and continue the march with steps taken straight forward without stiffness or exaggeration of movements. Swing the arms easily in their natural arcs, 6 inches to the front and 3 inches to the rear of the body. To halt when marching in quick time, the commands are: Squad HALT. At the command HALT, given as either foot strikes the ground, execute the halt in two counts by advancing and planting the other foot and then bringing up the foot in rear.

To Mark Time the commands are; Mark-Time, MARCH.

Being in march at the command MARCH, given as either foot strikes the ground, advance and plant the other foot, bring up the foot in rear, placing it so that both heels are on line and continue the cadence by alternately raising and planting each foot. The feet are raised 2 inches from the ground.

50

Being at a halt, at the command **MARCH,** raise and plant first the left then the · right as prescribed above.

The halt is executed from mark time as from quick time.

Half Step.—The commands are: Half Step **MARCH.** At the command **MARCH,** take steps of 15 inches in quick time. To resume the full step from the half step or mark time the commands are: Forward **MARCH.**

Side Step.—Being at a halt the commands are: Right (Left) Step **MARCH.** At the command **MARCH,** carry the right foot 12 inches to the right, place the left foot beside the right, left knee straight. Continue the cadence of quick time. (The side step is executed in quick time from the halt and for short distances only.)

Back Step.—Being at a halt the commands are, Backward **MARCH.** At the command **MARCH,** take steps, beginning with the left foot, 15 inches straight to the rear.

To March to the Flank.—Being in march the commands are: By The Right (Left) Flank— **MARCH.** At the command **MARCH,** given as the right (left) foot strikes the ground, advance and plant the left (right) foot, then face to the right (left) in marching and step off in the new direction.

Oblique March.—Being in march the commands are Right (Left) Oblique—**MARCH.** At the command **MARCH,** given as the right (left) foot strikes the ground, advance and plant the left (right) foot, then face to the right (left) oblique in marching and step off in the new direction.

To resume the original direction, the commands are—Forward, MARCH. At the command MARCH each individual faces half left (right) in marching then moves straight to the front.

Change Step.—The commands are Change Step, MARCH. Being in march at quick time, at the command MARCH, given as the right foot strikes the ground, advance and plant the left foot, plant the toe of the right foot near the heel of the left and step off with the left foot. (Execute the change on the right foot similarly, the command MARCH being given as the left foot strikes the ground.)

To the Rear.—To face to the rear in marching, being in march, the commands are: To The Rear, MARCH. At the command MARCH, given as the right foot strikes the ground, advance and plant the left foot, turn to the right about on the balls of both feet and immediately step off with the left foot.

Other Marchings.—March other than at Attention. The commands are: Route Step, MARCH or At Ease, MARCH. Route Step MARCH, at the command MARCH Volunteers are not required to march at attention or to maintain silence. At Ease, MARCH is the same as Route Step, MARCH, except that Volunteers will maintain silence.

Dismissing the Squad.—The unit being at a halt the leader calls the unit to attention, if they are not at attention, from a point six paces in front of the center of the unit. He then will give the command—DISMISSED. Volunteers are then free to go and do as they please until the next regularly scheduled drill period.

Forming the Platoon.

To form the platoon, which consists of 3 squads—the command, FALL IN will be given by the senior leader facing the area on which he wishes the platoon to form. At this command the unit will form facing the leader with its center 6 paces to his front in 3 parallel lines (each of these lines constitutes a squad). (Should there be insufficient men to form 3 complete squads, skeleton squads of as near equal number as possible will be formed in 3 ranks, squad leaders placing themselves directly behind one another.)

Fig. V.—A Platoon in Column of Squads

From this formation the unit can march; forward, to the right, or to the left.

Platoon Movements.

At the command: Forward MARCH, each man steps off with his left foot directly to his own front preserving his relative position and so regulates his step that the ranks remain parallel to his original front.

At the command: Right (Left) FACE Forward MARCH, the unit executes a right face on the heel of the right foot and ball of the left foot at the word FACE and at the word MARCH they step off with their left foot as in moving to the front. (Left face is performed by turning on the heel of the left foot and the ball of the right foot.) In the movements to the right or left the commander of the unit takes a position three paces in front of the left file of his command, at double time if necessary.

Being in a column to change direction the commands are—Column Right (Left) MARCH. At the command MARCH, given as the right (left) foot strikes the ground the first man of the leading element on the right (left) advances one step and then steps off in the new direction using half steps until the men to his left (right) are abreast of him. Full step is then resumed.

Close Interval—Normal Interval.—Being in column of threes at normal interval between squads to March or form at Close Interval, the commands are: Close, MARCH. At the command MARCH, the squads close to the center by obliquing until the interval between men is 4 inches. The center squad take up the half step until the dress has been regained.

If this movement is executed from the halt, the squads close toward the center by executing Right or Left Step until 4-inch intervals are reached.

Being in column of threes at close interval between squads to March or form at Normal Interval, the commands are: Extend, MARCH. At the command MARCH, the squads open to the right and left from the center by obliquing until the normal interval is regained.

If this movement is executed from the halt, the squads Right or Left Step until normal interval is regained.

Change Direction.—Being in column of threes to change direction, the commands are: Column Right (Left) MARCH. The right flank man of the leading rank is the pivot. At the command MARCH, given as the right foot strikes the ground, the right flank man of the leading rank faces to the right in marching and takes up the half step until the other men of his rank are abreast of him, then he resumes the full step. The other men of the leading rank oblique to the right in marching without changing interval, place themselves abreast of the pivot man, and conform to his step. The ranks in rear of the leading rank execute the movement on the same ground and in the same manner as the leading rank.

Fig. VI

Forming the Citizens' Defense Corps for Parade

(Services will form and move as platoons)

●	Mayor, Defense Coordinator and Dignitaries.
☐	Commander, C. D. C.
▭	Staff.
▭	Messengers.
▭	Drivers.
☐	Fire Department Chief.
▭	Auxiliary Firemen.
▭	Rescue Squads.
☐	Police Department Chief.
▭	Auxiliary Police.
▭	Bomb Squads.
☐	Colors.
☐	Warden Service Chief.
▭	Air Raid Wardens.
▭	Fire Watchers.
▭	Emergency Food Housing Units.
☐	Medical Service Chief.
▭	Medical Field Units.
▭	Nurses' Aides Corps.
☐	Public Works Service Chief.
▭	Demolition and Clearance Crews.
▭	Road Repair Squads.
▭	Decontamination Corps.

☆ U. S. GOVERNMENT PRINTING OFFICE : 1942 16—25743-1

www.ingramcontent.com/pod-product-compliance
Lightning Source LLC
Chambersburg PA
CBHW061158040426
42445CB00013B/1722